Let's Get Fit!

Activities to get kids moving and learning!

HighReach Learning®, Inc. is committed to creating high-quality, developmentally appropriate learning materials that facilitate a creative, integrated, hands-on learning experience for the whole child. Our goal is to enhance the development of readiness skills and encourage a love for learning in every young child.

Author: Beverly A. Warkulwiz
Editor: Tammy A. Willis
Copy Editor: Barbara C. Kirchner, Pamela R. Jarrell
Design and Layout: Nancy Rentschler
Illustrator: Deborah C. Johnson

Printed in the USA. All rights reserved.

ISBN 978-1-57332-465-6

Table of Contents

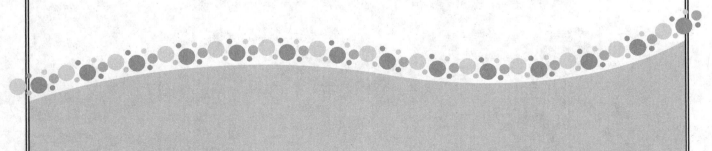

Introduction

Introduction

Just like cognitive skills, physical skills develop along a continuum throughout the early childhood years. In order to develop large and small muscles skills, children must have numerous opportunities to participate in a wide variety of movement activities.

What are large muscle skills?

Large muscle skills, also known as *gross motor* skills, can be broken down into three main developmental areas: *locomotor skills, stability skills,* and *manipulative skills.*

Locomotor skills are those in which the body moves from one location to another. You could further separate locomotor skills into two main types of activities. "Traveling" activities are designed for children to explore the many ways to get from here to there (e.g., walking, marching, leaping, skipping). "Chasing and fleeing" games, otherwise known as playing tag, combine traveling skills with the ability to quickly change direction and speed.

Stability skills, or *nonlocomotor* skills, are those in which the body generally remains in place but moves in other ways. Balancing, jumping and landing, dancing, and stretching are just a few examples of stability skills.

Manipulative skills, within the context of gross motor development, are developed through activities in which force is applied or received from objects. For example, tossing and catching a scarf, bouncing a ball, or kicking a beanbag into a box are activities that focus on manipulative skills.

What are small muscle skills?

Small muscle skills, or *fine motor* skills, can be thought of as "finger skills." Activities such as cutting and gluing paper, stacking blocks, pouring a drink, exploring playdough, and painting a picture help to develop fine motor skills. Many personal-care activities, such as tying shoes, buttoning a shirt, and zipping a coat, also help to refine small muscle skills.

What are developmentally appropriate movement experiences?

Developmentally appropriate movement experiences are child-centered in every way. As you begin to plan movement experiences for young children, you must take into account several variables. For each individual child, consider the following:

- What are the child's physical, cognitive, social, and emotional strengths and needs?
- In what types of previous movement experiences has the child participated?
- What is the child's age and body size?
- What are the child's interests? What motivates the child?
- Will the cultural background of the child affect his/her learning and participation in certain movement activities?

Simply stated, it is not appropriate to take a one-size-fits-all approach to planning movement experiences. Just as you would not expect all five year olds to know how to read, you should not expect all five years old to know how to skip. Differentiate activities so they are individually appropriate for each child. For example, if the focus of your lesson is bouncing a ball, some children may be ready to dribble the ball while walking forwards, but others may only be ready to drop and catch the ball while standing in place. This is not to say, however, that you shouldn't encourage the children to explore new skills or strive to attain proficiency of a skill. Small group instruction, child-selected activity stations, and free exploration of movement and materials will allow the children to feel challenged at a level that is "just right" for them.

My children have recess every day, isn't that enough?

Engaging in play is certainly an integral part of a child's physical, cognitive, social, and emotional development. It is essential to provide several opportunities for children to play each and every day. However, unstructured play should not account for your movement program in its entirety. Purposeful movement experiences should be integrated across the curriculum, both inside the classroom and on the playground. For example you could march in place as you say the days of the week, clap your hands as you count, or "dance" like the wind as you learn about weather.

Do we really need to worry about children "getting fit" at such a young age?

The importance of appropriate movement experiences for children is even more apparent now than it ever was before. With the prevalence of childhood obesity on the rise, establishing healthy habits in young children should be a top priority. Encourage these habits by reminding the children to wash their hands, brush their teeth, eat healthy foods, and keep their bodies moving and learning!

Resources

Bredekamp, S., & Copple, C. (Eds.). (1997). *Developmentally appropriate practice in early childhood programs* (Rev. ed.). Washington, DC: National Association for the Education of Young Children.

Dau, E. (1999). *Child's play: Revisiting play in early childhood settings.* Baltimore, MD: Paul H. Brooks Publishing Co.

Rampmeyer, K. (2000). *Appropriate practices in movement programs for young children ages 3-5.* Reston, VA: National Association for Sports and Physical Education.

Sanders, S. (2002). *Active for life: Developmentally appropriate movement programs for young children.* Washington, DC: National Association for the Education of Young Children.

Guidelines for Designing
Appropriate Movement Experiences

√   Plan daily activities that address the development of both gross motor and fine motor skills.

√   Differentiate activities based on children's strengths, needs, and interests.

√   Whenever possible, work with small groups of children to increase participation opportunities for every child.

√   Repeat activities frequently so children can explore new skills and begin to refine existing ones.

√   Integrate movement activities throughout all areas of the curriculum.

√   Provide numerous opportunities for children to engage in unstructured play, free exploration of movement and materials, planned movement activities, and organized cooperative games.
(Note: Competitive games are *not* appropriate for young children.)

√   Model a positive attitude toward fitness and nutrition to help young children develop healthy habits that will last a lifetime.

How To Use This Book

Well-planned movement experiences should keep the children at a constant level of moderate to vigorous activity. Throughout this book, you will find over 250 activities focusing on each of the main skills and sub-skills, conveniently organized by everyday classroom materials (balls, beanbags, jump ropes, hoops, etc.). Browse through each chapter and select one or more activities that the children will enjoy. Also included are helpful resources and reproducibles, such as the *National Standards for Physical Education* (pp. 86–89) and suggestions on how to easily create activity variations (p. 90).

Note: Some activities are designed for whole group participation, some for small group, and some can be either. Look for the (S) and (W) symbols to help you as you plan.

Locomotor Skills

Let's Get Fit!

Locomotor
Traveling

Walking, marching, running, hopping, galloping, leaping, and skipping are all ways to "travel" from here to there!

This Is the Way
(tune: "Here We Go Round the Mulberry Bush")

This is the way we hop on one foot,
Hop on one foot, hop on one foot.
This is the way we hop on one foot.
Oh, moving makes us healthy!

This is the way we gallop around...

This is the way we slide to the side...

This is the way we leap up high...

 ### Jump Ropes

Encourage the children to practice leaping around the room. To do this, take a few steps forward, push off with one foot, then land on the other foot. Lay two jump ropes on the floor about two feet apart and parallel to each other. Have children pretend that the area between the ropes is a stream. Invite the children to leap over the "stream" (ropes) and land on the other side. **S W**

Divide children into groups of four or five and have them stand in a single file line. Lay a jump rope on the floor in front of each group. At your signal, the children should pick up their ropes, run to the other end of the room, and pretend to put out a "fire" with their "hoses" (ropes). Encourage your little firefighters to work together as they run to the rescue! **W**

Let's Get Fit!

Jump Ropes

Provide each child with a jump rope. Ask the children to lay the jump ropes on the floor in a straight line. Model how to hop down the path, alternating feet as you go (hop right, hop left). Ⓢ

Hop, Hop, Hop

Right hop, left hop.
High hop, low hop.
Big hop, little hop.
Fast hop, slow hop.

So many ways to
Hop, hop, hop –
Please tell me how to
Stop, stop, stop!

Lay 5–6 jump ropes on the floor parallel to each other with about ten feet between each rope. Encourage the children to travel from the first jump rope to the last, changing the type of locomotor movement at each jump rope. Ⓢ

Use six jump ropes to form a large triangle with two ropes on each side. Invite the children to travel around the outside of the triangle in various ways (marching, hopping, galloping, etc.). Ⓢ

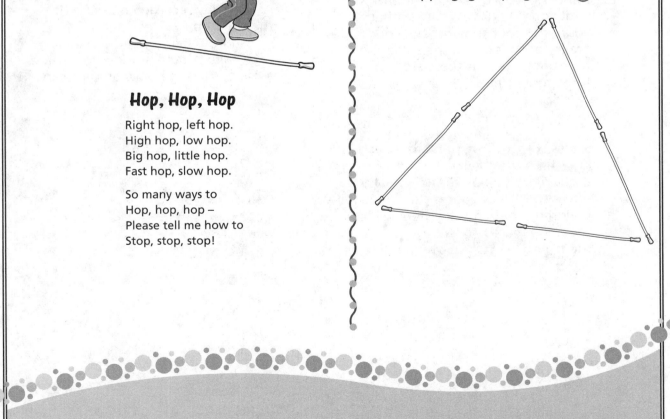

Hoops

Try this variation of the Chicken Dance. Provide each child with a hoop. Have children place their hoops on the floor and stand inside them. Play a recording of the traditional tune "The Chicken Dance." Encourage the children to do the chicken dance inside their hoops on the refrain, then slide-step around the outside of their hoops on each verse.

Note: How do you do the Chicken Dance? On each refrain – "quack" with your hands four times, "flap" your arms four times, shake your "tail" for four beats, then clap four times. Repeat these steps three more times. Ⓢ

Scatter red, yellow, and green hoops around the room (two of each color). Call out a red, yellow, or green fruit or vegetable. Children should quickly step inside the hoop matching the color of the fruit or vegetable you named. Ⓢ Ⓦ

Invite the children to play Hot Hoops. Lay 2–3 hoops of each available color on the floor spread several feet apart. Have children stand inside the hoops. (Two children may share the same hoop.) Begin by saying, "Red hoops are hot!" Children standing in red hoops should quickly move to a different colored hoop. Repeat, each time naming a different color. Ⓢ Ⓦ

Gather 8–12 children to play Musical Hoops. Lay six hoops on the floor to form a rectangle (shown below). As you play recorded music, invite the children to skip around the rectangle. When the music stops, each child should quickly step inside a hoop, sharing hoops as necessary. Ⓢ

Hoops

Enjoy the "hoop-la" that emerges from this friendly game. Lay one hoop of each available color on the floor spread several feet apart. Call out a color. Encourage each child to hop to the color hoop you named and place one foot inside the hoop. Repeat, each time naming a different color. **W**

Use this activity to help children develop an awareness of general and personal space. Invite each child to step inside a hoop and hold it around his/her waist. Encourage the children to move around the room without bumping into each other. At your signal, the children should drop their hoops to the floor and sit in them. Repeart several times. **S**

Divide children into two groups. Have one group stand side by side. Give each child in the line a hoop. Ask the children to hold the hoops upright (touching the ground) in front of their bodies to form a tunnel. Invite the other group of children to crawl through the hoop tunnel. Switch roles and repeat. **W**

In the center of the room, place 12 hoops in a circle on the floor and number them to resemble a clock. Give each child a number card from 1–12. Ask the children to stand around the perimeter of the room. At your signal, each child should run to the clock and stand in the hoop that matches the number on his/her card. Once all the children are in place, count together from 1 to 12. Collect the cards and play again. **W**

Beanbags

Scatter different colored beanbags at one end of the room (one per child) and place a row of matching colored hoops at the other end. Have children stand side by side in front of the hoops. At your signal, each child should move across the room, pick up one beanbag, travel back to the hoops, and place the beanbag in the matching hoop. Invite the children to scatter the beanbags again and continue to play, each time changing the type of locomotor movement. (S) (W)

Gather several red and blue beanbags. Give each child one beanbag. Have the children walk slowly around the room with their beanbags. At your signal, the children should stop moving and listen closely to your directions. Tell the children holding the red beanbags to travel in a given way and the children holding the blue beanbags to travel in a different way. For example, you might say, "Red beanbags leap and blue beanbags tiptoe." Repeat, each time asking the children to travel around the room in different way.

Note: You can use beanbags of any color, but limit it to two colors for this activity. (S)

Use beanbags to form a large square on the floor. Invite the children to move around the square as desired. At your signal, the children should stop, change direction and type of movement, then continue moving around the square. (S)

Travel Here and Travel There
(tune: "London Bridge")

Travel here and travel there.
We can travel anywhere.
We can run and skip and hop.
We can go and we can stop.

Beanbags

Place at least one beanbag per child on the floor spread several feet apart. Invite the children to travel around the room. At your signal, the children should step on the nearest beanbag and freeze. Repeat, each time asking them to travel around the room in a different way. (S)(W)

Skip to My Lou
(tune: Traditional)

Lou, lou, skip to my lou.
Lou, lou, skip to my lou.
Lou, lou, skip to my lou.
Skip to my lou my darling.

Lou, lou, leap to my lou.
Lou, lou, leap to my lou.
Lou, lou, leap to my lou.
Leap to my lou my darling.

Lou, lou, hop to my lou.
Lou, lou, hop to my lou.
Lou, lou, hop to my lou.
Hop to my lou my darling.

Lou, lou, gallop to my lou…

Lou, lou, stomp to my lou…

Lou, lou, march to my lou…

Place different colored beanbags on the floor spread several feet apart. Have children stand side by side on a starting line. Hold up a number card from 1–5 and call out a color. The objective is for the children to travel around the room, touch the appropriate number of beanbags that match the identified color, then return to the starting line. Repeat, each time traveling around the room in a different way. (S)(W)

Create a long, straight line of beanbags on the floor. Invite the children to hop along the right side of the beanbag pathway and walk backwards along the left side. Repeat to form a continuous loop. (S)

Parachutes

Assign a number from 1–5 to each child. Invite the children to stand around a parachute, holding it with both hands. Call out a number. Children whose number you named should run around the parachute then return to their original spots. While this is happening, the rest of the children should shake the parachute. Repeat, each time calling out a different number. Ⓦ

Divide children into two groups. Ask one group of children to kneel around a parachute and hold it with two hands. The other group should form a single file line and crawl under the parachute. Once all the children have crawled to the other side, switch roles and repeat.

Note: You may want to do this activity during Fire Prevention Month (October), as a way to practice crawling "under smoke" to escape. Ⓦ

Challenge the children to move the parachute from one side of the room or playground to the other. Cooperation is the key! Ⓦ

Other Materials

Invite the children to travel around the room as you play recorded music. When the music stops, the children should freeze. Repeat, changing the type of movement each time. Ⓦ

On separate sheets of paper, write a numeral with which the children are familiar and label containers to match. Loosely crumple each sheet of paper into a ball. Scatter the paper balls at one end of the room and place the numbered containers at the other end. Have children stand side by side in front of the containers. At your signal, each child should move across the room, pick up one paper ball, open the paper to reveal the numeral, then place the paper in the appropriate container. Invite the children to crumple and scatter the paper, then play again. Each time you play, change the type of movement to develop the children's locomotor skills. Ⓢ Ⓦ

Practice the slide-step across the room in one direction then the other (slide to the right, then slide to the left). Play recorded music and slide-step to the beat. Change direction every eight counts. Ⓢ Ⓦ

Provide each child with a scarf. Tell the children to hold one end of their scarves above their heads, travel around the room, and watch how the scarves wave in the breeze. Every so often, ask the children to travel around the room in a different way. Ⓢ Ⓦ

Draw straight, curvy, and zigzag pathways on the pavement with chalk. Have children move along the pathways, each time traveling in a different way. Ⓢ Ⓦ

Ask the children to form a single file line. Play a recording of a march (e.g., "The Stars and Stripes Forever" by John Philip Sousa) and invite the children to march in their very own parade! Ⓦ

Other Materials

Label the corners of the room with different colors, shapes, letters, or numerals. As you play recorded music, invite the children to skip around the room. When the music stops, each child should move to the nearest corner. Call out a corner by color, shape, etc., and have the children in the named corner come to the center of the room. As you play the music again, the children in the center should dance in place as the rest of the children skip around the room. Continue to play until all of the children are dancing in the center of the room. Ⓦ

Beat a steady rhythm on a drum. Invite the children to walk or march on each beat. Vary the tempo of the rhythm to help children develop good listening and locomotor skills. Ⓢ Ⓦ

Gather two medium-sized boxes. Label one box "Healthy Food" and the other box "Junk Food." Encourage the children to share what they know about healthy food and junk food. Scatter several pieces of plastic play food around the room (at least one food per child). Each child should travel around the room, pick up one piece of play food, and place it in the appropriate box. Once all the items have been sorted, talk about the foods in each box. Remind the children that their bodies need healthy foods to help them think, play, and grow. Ⓢ

Ask the children to stand in a single file line and place their hands gently on the shoulders of the person in front of them. Play a recording of "The Bunny Hop" and invite the children to dance to the music.

Note: How do you do the Bunny Hop? Take six alternating steps forward – step left, right foot out; step right, left foot out. Repeat pattern two more times... then hop, hop, hop! Ⓦ

Other Materials

Gather a small set of percussion instruments with distinct sounds (e.g., rhythm sticks, maracas, bongos). For each instrument, choose a different movement for the children to explore. For example, the children could walk to the steady beat of the rhythm sticks, wiggle across the room as you shake the maracas, and stomp to the beat of the bongos. Vary the instruments and tempos to help children develop good listening and locomotor skills. (S)(W)

Play a recording of "The William Tell Overture" by Gioacchino Rossini. Encourage the children to gallop like horses to the music. From time to time, instruct children to alternate their lead foot (front foot). (W)

No Materials

Invite two children of similar height to face each other and create a bridge with their arms by clasping their hands together. Encourage the children to sing "London Bridge" as they travel around the room and under the bridge in a large loop. Repeat, each time changing the type of movement and inviting two new children to become the bridge. (S)(W)

Invite the children to move like different animals. They could stomp like elephants, gallop like horses, waddle like ducks, or hop like frogs. Explain that like us, many animals need to "exercise" (move) to stay healthy. (W)

Call out a color. Encourage the children to travel around the room, touching things that are the same color. Repeat, each time choosing a different color and way to travel around the room. (S)(W)

Traveling

 No Materials

Integrate math and fitness by playing How Many Steps Before the King/Queen? Ask children to stand side by side. Stand at least 30 feet away on a line parallel with the children. The children should ask, "How many steps before the king/queen?" Respond with a number from 1–10 and specify tiny, medium, or giant steps (e.g., six giant steps). Repeat until all of the children have reached the line on which you are standing.

Note: It is best if the teacher assumes the role of the king or queen to maximize movement opportunities for the children. (W)

Divide children into groups of three or four. The children in each group should stand in a circle and hold hands to become a "bubble." Each bubble should move around the room in a slow spinning motion without touching any other bubbles. (W)

Caution: Do this activity in a large, open space so the children can move about safely.

Tell the children to imagine that the room is a large swamp. Ask children to describe how they would move through a swamp and what it might feel like. Invite the children to trudge "across the swamp" (from one end of the room to the other). Each time you cross the swamp, have children pretend that the swamp is filled with something different and move accordingly (e.g., deep snow, marbles, eggs, tall grass, bubble gum, oil). (S)(W)

No Materials

Encourage the children to move around the room, representing various forms of transportation. The children could fly like a plane, row a boat, ride a bike, or choo choo down the track!

Invite the children to tiptoe and stomp around the room. You may want to signal the movements with a single clap for tiptoeing and two loud stomps for stomping. Ⓦ

Make a set of matching cards with letters, numbers, or shapes. Give one card to each child. Ask children to keep what is on the card a secret until you begin to play the game. At your signal, encourage the children to move around the room to find their partners (children whose cards match). Collect the cards and play again, each time asking children to travel around the room in a different way. Ⓢ Ⓦ

Talk about traffic lights and what the colors mean. Ask children to stand side by side. Stand at least 30 feet away on a line parallel with the children. When you say, "Green light!" the children should shout "Go!" and quickly walk toward you. When you say, "Red light!" the children should shout "Stop!" and then freeze. Continue until all of the children have traveled to the line on which you are standing. Ⓦ

Have the children explore different kinds of steps – big and little, light and heavy, tired and excited, happy and sad, and so forth. You may also want to encourage the children to try walking forwards, backwards, and sideways. Ⓦ

Invite the children to move around the room in a way of their choice. At your signal, the children should choose a different way to move around the room. Ⓢ Ⓦ

Locomotor
Chasing & Fleeing

Chasing and fleeing games (tag) combine traveling skills with the ability to quickly change direction and speed.

Come Let's Run!
(tune: "Do Your Ears Hang Low?")

Come let's run, run, run!
Let's all run and have some fun.
Can you chase? Can you flee?
Can you run away from me?
We can play. We can tag.
We can zig and we can zag.
Come let's run, run, run!

 ## Parachutes

Try this fun variation of Duck, Duck, Goose. Select one child to be *It*. Have the rest of the children kneel around a parachute and hold onto it with both hands. *It* should walk around the circle and say "Duck" as he/she lightly taps each child on the shoulder. When *It* taps a child and says "Goose," the tapped child should chase *It* around the parachute and try to tag *It* before *It* sits down in the empty spot. As *It* is being chased, the rest of the children should shake the parachute in a controlled manner. If *It* sits down before being tagged, the other child becomes *It*. Ⓦ

Spread out a parachute on the floor in the center of the room. At your signal, the children should run around the room. Call out a color that is on the parachute. The objective is for the children to touch the named color on the parachute before the teacher tags them. Ⓢ Ⓦ

Beanbags

Choose a few children to be *It* and give each one of them a beanbag. At your signal, the children who are *It* should chase the other children. Once a child is tagged, *It* gives the tagged child the beanbag and he/she is now *It*. Ⓦ

. . . .

Tag, Tag, Tag, You're It!
(tune: "Row, Row, Row Your Boat")

Tag, tag, tag, you're It!
Now you follow me.
Try to catch me if you can.
I'll run away and flee!

Scatter 5–6 beanbags on the floor spread several feet apart. Select a few children to be *It*. At your signal, the children who are *It* should chase the other children. If a child places one foot on a beanbag he/she is "safe."

Note: No child should stay on a beanbag for too long, and *It* should not wait for a child to leave a beanbag. Ⓦ

. . . .

For this game, the teacher is *It*. Provide each child with a beanbag. The children should hold their beanbags in their hands as they run away from *It*. Once tagged, each child should walk around the room balancing the beanbag on his/her head. Continue to play until all of the children have been tagged.

Note: If the beanbag falls off a child's head, he/she should replace it and continue to walk. Ⓦ

Chasing & Fleeing

Other Materials

Choose two children to be *It*. As you play recorded music, the children who are *It* chase and tag the other children. Once tagged, the children freeze. Stop the music about a minute later. The children who are frozen are now *It*. Play the music again and continue the game. Ⓦ

Record several short excerpts of instrumental music, alternating the selections by tempo (slow music and fast music). Divide children into pairs. One child in each pair will chase, and the other will flee. Play the music and encourage the children to listen closely. When the music is slow both children should walk slowly, and when it's fast they should run. Once *It* tags his/her partner, the children should switch roles. Ⓢ Ⓦ

Invite the children to play Pebbles, a tag game from Greece. One child is *It* and holds a small pebble in his/her hand. The rest of the players stand side by side and put one hand out, palm up. *It* walks down the line, pretending to place the pebble in each person's hand. Whomever *It* gives the pebble to must race *It* to the base (a location chosen before the game begins). If *It* gets there first, the player who received the pebble is now *It*.

Note: To foster cultural awareness and appreciation, incorporate games from other countries into your lessons. (See also "Catch the Tail" on page 28.) Ⓦ

Other Materials

Take the children outside on a sunny (and not too windy) day. Use a battery-operated bubble machine to blow large amounts of bubbles. Invite the children to chase the bubbles and pop them. Ⓢ Ⓦ

Provide each child with a scarf. Help the children tuck the scarves into the necklines of their shirts (in the back). At the beginning of this game, the teacher assumes the role of *It* and chases the children. Instead of tagging the children, *It* tries to remove the scarves from the children's shirts. Once a child has been "tagged," he/she also becomes *It*. Continue to play until all of the children have been tagged. Ⓢ Ⓦ

Caution: Supervise the children carefully during this activity. Remind them to pull the scarves gently.

 ## Hoops

Place a hoop in the center of the room. Divide children into four groups and assign each group a color. The children in each group become a "fish family" (e.g., red fish family, blue fish family). The teacher assumes the role of the "fisherman" and tries to "catch" (tag) the fish as they swim away from him/her. Once the fisherman catches a fish, he/she puts the fish in the "bucket" (hoop) then tries to catch another one. When the fisherman is not looking (intentionally), the fish's family rescues the fish from the bucket and the fish is free to swim again. Ⓦ

Invite the children to play Dock the Spaceship. Provide each child with a hoop. Each child should step inside the hoop and hold it around his/her waist. Tell children to imagine that they are the pilots of their very own spaceships (hoops). The teacher should chase the children as they "fly through space" (safely running with their hoops without bumping into each other). Once tagged, the children should "dock their spaceships" (sit inside the hoop) until they are "refueled" (another child taps them on the shoulder so they can rejoin the game). Ⓦ

Chasing & Fleeing

 ## No Materials

Invite the children to play Cat and Mouse. At the beginning of the game, the teacher pretends to be a cat and the children pretend to be mice (squeak and run with tiny steps). The "mice" should scatter around the room and flee from the "cat." As each child is tagged, he/she also becomes a cat (meows and shows "claws"). Continue to play until all of the mice have been caught.  W

Invite the children to play Catch the Tail, a tag game from China. Have the children form a single file line to become a "dragon," gently holding onto the shoulders of the person in front of them. The "head" of the dragon (first person) tries to catch its "tail" (last person) without breaking the line. Once the head catches the tail or if the line breaks, the first person moves to the back of the line and you play again.

Note: To foster cultural awareness and appreciation, incorporate games from other countries into your lessons. (See also "Pebbles" on page 26.) W

In this tag game, the children tiptoe, spin, or leap around the room like graceful ballerinas as they flee from *It*. Select a few children to be *It*. At your signal, the children who are *It* chase the ballet dancers. Once a child is tagged, he/she becomes *It* and the child who was *It* dances away. S

Dance and Spin
(tune: "Twinkle, Twinkle, Little Star")

Dance and spin so gracefully.
Dance and spin around like me.
Dance upon your tippytoes.
Dance so fast and dance so slow.
Dance and spin so gracefully.
Dance and spin around like me.

No Materials

Choose two different traveling skills – one for the children who are *It* and one for those who are fleeing. For example, children who are chasing could skip while children who are fleeing could leap. Once a child is tagged, he/she also becomes *It* and chases the others in the designated way. Ⓢ Ⓦ

Invite the children to play Fishing Frenzy. At the beginning of this tag game, the teacher pretends to be a fisherman and the children pretend to be fish (wiggle hands at sides like fins). The "fish" should swim around the room, trying not to get "caught" (tagged) by the "fisherman." As each child is tagged, he/she also becomes a fisherman and tries to catch some fish. Continue to play until all of the fish have been caught. Ⓦ

For this game, the teacher assumes the role of *It* and chases the children. Once *It* tags a child, the tagged child must "freeze" (stand still) with his/her legs open. Frozen players can rejoin the game after another player crawls between his/her legs. Ⓦ

I Love to Play Tag!

I love to play tag
With all of my friends.
I love to play tag,
The fun never ends.
I love to play tag,
To chase and to flee.
I love to play tag –
Please play tag with me!

Chasing & Fleeing

 No Materials

Divide children into pairs to play this game of Shadow Tag. One child in each pair will chase, and one will flee. Show the children how to "tag" their partners by jumping on their shadows. Once the child who is *It* "catches" the other person's shadow, the children switch roles. Ⓢ Ⓦ

Invite one child to be the first *It* in this cooperative tag game called Chain Link. After *It* tags another child, the two children link arms and work together to tag more children. Each child who is tagged also links onto the growing chain of children. Continue to play until only one child remains. Ⓦ

Select a few children to be *It*. At your signal, the children who are *It* should chase the other children. Once tagged, children should hop in place until tapped on the shoulder by another child so they may rejoin the game. Ⓦ

Select a few children to be cowboys and/or cowgirls. These children are *It* while the rest of the children pretend to be horses and gallop around the room. The cowboys/girls run (not gallop) and try to "round up the horses" (tag the other children). Once a child is tagged, he/she also becomes a cowboy/girl. Continue to play until all the horses have been rounded up. Yee-haw! Ⓦ

No Materials

Share the rhyme "Mr. Crocodile" with the children and encourage them to join in. Repeat a few times, then invite the children to play a tag game based on the rhyme.

At the beginning of this game, the teacher pretends to be a crocodile and the children pretend to be monkeys. (Making monkey movements and sounds) the "monkeys" should scatter around the room and flee from the "crocodile." As each child is tagged, he/she also becomes a crocodile (using arms to "snap" at the monkeys). Continue to play until all of the monkeys have been caught. (W)

Mr. Crocodile
(traditional fingerplay, revised)

Five little monkeys sitting in a tree,
Teasing Mr. Crocodile –
"You can't catch me!"
Along comes Mr. Crocodile
As quiet as can be and…
SNAPS one monkey right out of that tree!

Four little monkeys…
(Three… Two… One…)

No more monkeys sitting in a tree,
Teasing Mr. Crocodile –
"You can't catch me!"
Away swims Mr. Crocodile
As full as he can be…
"Now no more monkeys
will be teasing me!"

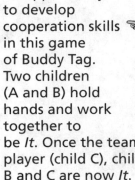

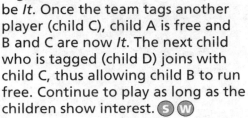

Children have an opportunity to develop cooperation skills in this game of Buddy Tag. Two children (A and B) hold hands and work together to be *It*. Once the team tags another player (child C), child A is free and B and C are now *It*. The next child who is tagged (child D) joins with child C, thus allowing child B to run free. Continue to play as long as the children show interest. (S) (W)

Select one child to be Mr. Wolf. Have the rest of the children stand side by side about 30 feet away from Mr. Wolf. Ask Mr. Wolf to turn around so he is facing the other way. The children ask, "What time is it Mr. Wolf?" and Mr. Wolf responds, "It is ___ o'clock" (fill in the hour). For every hour that is given, the children take that many steps toward Mr. Wolf. At some point, Mr. Wolf should respond, "It's dinnertime!" then turn around and chase the children back to the starting line. If Mr. Wolf successfully tags a child, that child assumes the role of Mr. Wolf.

Note: Substitute Miss, Mrs., or Ms. for Mr. as appropriate. (S) (W)

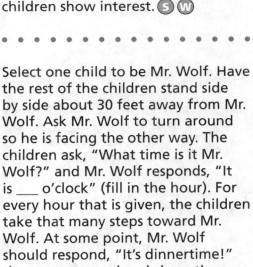

Stability Skills

Stability
Balancing

Balance is the ability to maintain your posture while moving or remaining still.

Can You Balance?
(tune: "Did You Ever See a Lassie?")

Can you balance on your right foot,
Your right foot, your right foot?
Can you balance on your right foot
Without falling down?
Lean this way and that way,
And this way and that way.
Can you balance on your right foot
Without falling down?

Can you balance on your left foot…

Can you balance with your eyes closed…

Balls

Provide each child with a large firm ball, such as a basketball. Have children place the ball on the floor. The objective is to use various body parts (e.g., finger, hand, elbow, knee, foot, head) to prevent the ball from moving. (S)

Invite each child to balance a tennis ball on a racket or the palm of one hand. Challenge the children to try walking forwards and backwards while balancing the ball. (S) (W)

This task may seem simple at first, but it requires a great deal of balance and concentration. Give each child 3–5 balls of various sizes (e.g., racquetball, tennis ball, football, kickball). Encourage the children to hold all the balls at the same time without dropping them. (S)

Jump Ropes

Provide each child with a jump rope. Ask the children to lay their jump ropes in a straight line on the floor. Have them pretend that they are in the circus, walking along a tightrope. To add an extra-special touch, you may want to play a recording of circus music in the background or sing the song below. (S) (W)

I'm a Tightrope Walker
(tune: "I'm a Little Teapot")

I'm a tightrope walker, look at me.
I can walk with balance, watch and see.
High up in the air, far from the ground,
In the circus I am found.

Divide children into pairs. Give each pair a jump rope to stretch out on the floor. One child should stand on each side of the rope, opposite his/her partner. Challenge the children to stand on one foot, using their partners to help them balance. (S) (W)

Stretch out a long jump rope on the floor. Tell children to imagine that the jump rope is a bridge across a river. Invite the children to walk across the "bridge" without falling into the "river" (area on either side of the jump rope). (S)

Balancing

 ## Beanbags

Provide each child with a beanbag. Have the children try to balance beanbags on various body parts (e.g., palm of hand, back of hand, arm, head, top of foot). Ⓢ Ⓦ

Scatter beanbags on the floor with varying distances between them (but still close enough for children to step from one to the next). Invite the children to move along the beanbag path as if they were stepping on stones across a pond. Ⓢ

Use this silly activity to practice balancing skills in a fun (and funny) way. Give each child a beanbag. Tell the children to place the beanbags between their knees and "walk" to a designated location. Ⓢ Ⓦ

Place a beanbag on the floor in front of each child. Call out a body part (e.g., toe, knee, elbow). Encourage each child to rest the named body part on his/her beanbags without falling over. Repeat, each time calling out a different body part. Ⓢ Ⓦ

Provide each child with a beanbag. Invite the children to balance their beanbags on their heads as they move around the room. Challenge the children to walk both forwards and backwards. Ⓢ Ⓦ

Give each child a beanbag and a wooden paint stick. Begin by encouraging the children to balance the beanbags on their paint sticks. Next, divide children into pairs. One child should balance the beanbag on his/her stick then try to pass it off to his/her partner without touching it. The children should pass the beanbags back and forth several times. Ⓢ Ⓦ

Other Materials

Draw large shapes, letters, or numbers on the pavement with chalk. Invite the children to demonstrate balance as they walk along each drawing. Ⓢ Ⓦ

Provide each child with a plastic spoon and a plastic egg (taped closed). Ask children to stand side by side on a starting line. The objective is for the children to balance the eggs on their spoons as they walk to a specified location and back to the line on which they began. Ⓢ Ⓦ

Have children practice walking in a straight line by placing one foot directly in front of the other. Encourage the children to experiment with various arm positions to help them balance even better. Ⓢ Ⓦ

Create a large square with masking tape on the floor (or draw one on the pavement with chalk). Invite the children to stand inside the square on one foot. Encourage the children to help each other balance inside the square as long as they are able. Next, have the children stand along the perimeter of the square and repeat the challenge. Ⓢ

Challenge each child to balance a quarter on one fingertip. If this task seems too easy for some children, encourage them to balance their quarters while walking across the room.

Note: Do not use play money for this activity because the "quarters" don't have enough weight. Ⓢ Ⓦ

Give each child a paper plate. Encourage the children to walk across the room balancing the plates on their heads. Ⓢ Ⓦ

Balancing

No Materials

This activity is not only fun to do, it's fun to watch! Invite the children to spin in circles as they count to ten. Once they count to ten, the children should stop spinning and try to stand still with balance. Ⓢ Ⓦ

Caution: Do this activity in a large, open space so the children can move about safely.

Challenge the children to develop balance and cooperation skills as they do the Spider Walk. Divide children into groups of four. Ask children to stand back to back in a circle, link arms, and count how many legs there are in all. Tell the children to pretend that they are spiders, which have eight legs. Invite the children to practice "walking like spiders" as they move around the room. Allow the children some time to explore freely, then give each "spider" a task to complete (e.g., moving to a particular location). Ⓢ Ⓦ

Caution: Do this activity in a large, open space so the children can move about safely.

Yoga helps to develop an inner sense of balance. Invite the children to try this balancing pose, or *asana* (AH-sah-nah), called "The Tree." Stand on your preferred foot. Place the bottom of your other foot against the inside of the leg just below the knee. Raise your arms above your head and relax your shoulders. Hold this position as long as you are able. Ⓢ Ⓦ

No Materials

Invite the children to travel around the room any way they choose (e.g., skip, run, leap, gallop). At your signal, the children should freeze and balance themselves as they hold still in their "frozen" positions. Ⓦ

Divide children into pairs. Each pair of children should sit back to back and link arms. Encourage the children to stand up by working cooperatively. After a while, invite successful pairs to explain how they accomplished the task. Ⓦ

Encourage each child to try balancing on his/her preferred foot. Have the children experiment with various arm positions above their heads, out to the sides, tucked like wings, out in front, and straight down at sides. Which arm position best helps them balance? Ⓢ

Ask the children to try balancing on their least preferred foot (e.g., right-handed children should try standing on their left foot). Have the children count to see how long they can stand on that foot, each time trying to balance a bit longer. Ⓢ Ⓦ

Balancing

No Materials

Encourage the children to stand with their feet together and their arms down at their sides. After 20–30 seconds, ask the children to close their eyes but remain in the same position. Next, have the children open their eyes and try to walk by placing one foot directly in front of the other. Repeat, this time with eyes closed. After both sets of movements are complete, ask the children if they think it's easier to balance with their eyes open or closed. Ⓢ

Balancing

Balancing is hard to do.
But let me share a clue or two.
Place one foot in front of the other.
Take one step, and then another.
Put your arms out to the sides.
Look straight ahead – don't close your eyes.

Have each child stand with his/her back against a wall. Tell the children to slide down the wall until it looks like they are sitting. Challenge the children to balance themselves in this position as long as they can. Ⓢ

Parachutes

Have the children stand around a parachute and practice lifting the parachute to the following positions (heights): toes (floor), knees, hips, nose, above head. Encourage the children to lift the parachute using a palms-down hold (thumbs below) and a palms-up hold (thumbs above). Ⓦ

Challenge the children to pick up a parachute with their backs towards it. Begin by bending one knee to the floor, grasp the parachute, and then stand holding the parachute at your hips using a palms-up hold (thumbs above). Ⓦ

Spread out a parachute on the floor. Invite the children, one at a time, to walk from one side of the parachute to the other along a seam. As each child is walking, the rest of the children should gently shake the parachute with two hands. Ⓦ

Hoops

Is it easier to balance with your feet together or spread widely apart? Give each child a hoop. Challenge the children to spin the hoop around their wrist, upper arm, and waist as they experiment with each stance. Ⓢ

Caution: Do this activity in a large, open space so the children can move about safely.

Divide children into groups of three or four and provide each group with a sturdy hoop. Ask children to sit around the hoop and hold onto it with both hands. The objective is to work together and stand up by pulling gently (and equally) on the hoop. Ⓢ Ⓦ

Provide each child with a hoop. Invite the children to rest their hoops on the floor (vertically), hold onto them with one hand, and balance on one foot. If this task is too easy for some children, encourage them to try raising one leg behind their bodies. Ⓢ Ⓦ

Stability
Jumping & Landing

Although jumping by itself could be considered a traveling skill, the ability to land with balance makes it a stability skill.

Jump to Ten

1 jump, 2 jumps, 3 jumps, 4…
Watch me jump and jump some more!

5 jumps, 6 jumps, 7 jumps, 8…
Jumping makes me feel so great!

9 jumps, 10 jumps, that's the end…
Let's jump, and jump, and jump again!

 No Materials

Encourage the children to freely explore jumping and landing. Can they jump and land on two feet? Jump with two feet but land on one foot? Jump with one foot but land on the other foot? There are a variety of ways that children can experiment with jumping and landing techniques. Ⓢ Ⓦ

Jumping high and jumping far are variations of this stability skill. To help children learn how to jump high, encourage them to bend their knees and spring upward with energy (not forward). To help children learn how to jump far, show them how to swing their arms back before the jump then use their arms to propel them as they jump forward (not up). Ⓢ Ⓦ

Begin by having all the children stand and face the same direction. Encourage the children to jump up, pivot to the side (90°), and land on two feet. Next, have the children jump up, pivot to the back (180°), and land on two feet. Finally, challenge the children to jump up, pivot all the way around (360°), and land on two feet. Repeat each jump several times in both directions (clockwise and counterclockwise) before moving onto the next jump. Ⓢ Ⓦ

Let's Get Fit!

Jump Ropes

Lay a jump rope on the floor in a straight line. Invite the children to jump over the rope and land on two feet. After several repetitions, challenge the children to jump with both feet in a zigzag pattern over the rope. Ⓢ

Gather four children to play Jump the Snake. Two children should hold the rope and wiggle it close to the ground like a snake, while the other children jump over the "snake" several times. Switch roles and repeat. Ⓢ

In this activity, two children slowly swing a jump rope from side to side and close to the ground. As they do this, another child attempts to jump on the rope to stop it (not jump over it).

Note: In addition to balance, this activity helps develop coordination and a sense of timing. Ⓢ

Other Materials

Give each child a hoop. Encourage the children to jump in and out of their hoops as you play recorded music in the background. Each time you stop the music, the children should freeze and maintain balance. Play the music and invite the children to jump again. Ⓢ Ⓦ

Set up sturdy platforms of various heights around the room. Invite the children to jump down from the platforms and land on two feet. Remind them to bend their knees slightly when they land. Ⓢ Ⓦ

Caution: Do not use platforms higher than two feet.

Ask the children to form a circle then turn off the lights. Stand in the middle of the circle. Using a powerful flashlight, move the beam of light around the circle and low to the ground. Encourage the children to jump over the light as it comes to them. Ⓢ Ⓦ

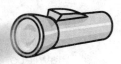

Stability
Dancing, Stretching, & More!

Twisting, turning, bending, and swaying are all ways to "stretch" children's stability skills!

Reach Up High
(tune: "This Old Man")

Reach up high, touch the ground.
Bend both ways then turn around.
If you exercise then you will see
Just how healthy you can be!

Stretching high, stretching low.
Dancing on my tippytoes.
If you exercise then you will see
Just how healthy you can be!

 ### Scarves

Encourage the children to use their scarves in imaginative ways. For example, they could pretend to go fishing, sweep the floor, tie their shoes, and so forth. The children could also move their scarves like eagles soaring in the sky, butterflies fluttering from flower to flower, or snakes slithering on the ground. Through this creative movement activity, the children can really "stretch" their imaginations as well as their bodies! Ⓢ Ⓦ

Play recorded music as the children dance freely with scarves. You may want to record excerpts of music with varying tempos and moods to maximize opportunities for creativity and expression. Ⓢ Ⓦ

Scarves

Use this activity to reinforce the concepts of up, down, left, and right. Provide each child with a scarf. Stand facing the children and say the appropriate directional word as you perform each movement. Encourage the children to mirror what you say and do.

Note: When you say "left" be sure to move your scarf to the right (and vice versa). Why? Since the children are looking at you, your left and right actions are opposite theirs. Ⓢ Ⓦ

Provide each child with a scarf. Invite the children to "write" letters or numbers by moving their scarves through the air. Ⓢ

Invite the children to "draw" shapes in the air with their scarves. Can they make a small circle and large circle? Can they make a triangle and a square? Work together to discover how many different shapes you can "draw" with scarves. Ⓢ Ⓦ

Beanbags

Lay a beanbag on the floor in front of each child. The objective is to pick up the beanbag using various body parts (e.g., hands, feet, knees, two fingers). To accomplish this challenging task, the children may need to sit or lay down. Ⓢ Ⓦ

Divide children into pairs. Provide each pair with a beanbag. Challenge the children to pass the beanbag to their partners using any body parts except their mouths or hands. Ⓢ Ⓦ

Provide each child with one red beanbag and one blue beanbag. Ask the children to hold the red beanbags in their right hands and the blue beanbags in their left hands. (Hint: <u>R</u>ed <u>R</u>ight) Give directions that involve touching each beanbag to a specific location on the body (e.g., put the red beanbag on your knee, put the blue beanbag on your head).

Note: You can use other colored beanbags, but every child must have the same two colors and hold them in the same hands. Ⓢ

Dancing, Stretching, & More!

Parachutes

Encourage the children to work together as they lift and lower a parachute from their toes to above their heads, and back down again. Try lifting the parachute with both slow and quick movements. (W)

• • • • • • • • • •

Sing the song "Head, Shoulders, Knees, and Toes" together as the children move the parachute to the named position on the body. When you sing "Eyes and ears and mouth and nose," take four steps around the circle. (W)

• • • • • • • • • •

Ask the children to stand with their backs toward the parachute and hold it with their palms up (thumbs above). Encourage the children to lunge forward with one leg, stretch for a count of five, then step back into place. Use the cues *lunge*, *stretch*, and *relax* to guide the children during this activity. (W)

• • • • • • • • • •

Play recordings of music from a variety of genres. Encourage the children to move the parachute to the rhythm and/or mood of the music. (W)

Move a parachute in various ways. For example, try moving it with fast and slow shakes, or large and small waves. Raise the parachute high and bring it low to the ground as you explore each type of movement. (W)

• • • • • • • • • •

Have the children quickly lift the parachute high above their heads. Take a few steps towards the center to make an "umbrella," then walk back out. To make a "volcano," lift the parachute again, take a few steps in, and quickly pull it down to the floor. If the children would like to sit in an "igloo," lift the parachute, take a few steps in, pull it down behind you (while still facing the center), and sit on the edge. (W)

Parachutes

Invite the children to stand around the parachute and lift it using a palms-down hold (thumbs below). When you lift the parachute together, everyone should happily say "Good Morning!" Lower the parachute to the floor and sit with your legs under it. Once the children are settled, everyone should whisper "Good night," and snuggle under the parachute like a blanket. Ⓦ

Encourage the children to hold the parachute tightly with palms down (thumbs below). Challenge them to pass the parachute around the circle while standing in place. Ⓦ

Play a recording of fun dance music in the background. Invite three children at a time to dance on the parachute in the center. As the children are dancing, the rest of the children should gently shake the parachute. Ⓦ

No Materials

Invite each child to independently make letter shapes with his/her body on the floor. A few easy letters to try are: C, F, J, and X. Next, divide children into pairs. Challenge the children to work cooperatively to form more letter shapes. Some letters that work well with two people are: A, D, H, L, M, T, V, W, and Y. Ⓢ

In this game, the Leader (teacher or child) gives a direction emphasizing various stability skills for all the children to follow (e.g., touch your toes, lunge forward, bend from side to side). From time to time, the Leader should shout "Statues," at which point everyone should freeze like a statue. Ⓦ

Divide children into groups of four or five. Each child in turn should stretch, twist, or bend in a unique way. The objective is for the children to perform an action that no one else in their group has done. Ⓦ

Dancing, Stretching, & More!

 No Materials

When you call out "Daytime!" the children should dance, wiggle, twirl, stretch, and so forth. When you whisper "Nighttime!" the children should lie down and pretend to sleep. **W**

Invite the children to play Copycat. In this activity, the Leader (teacher or child) performs an action, such as dancing, stretching, twisting, bending, or swaying. The children should copy each action performed by the Leader.

Note: Remember to focus on stability skills, not locomotor skills. **S** **W**

Encourage the children to act out various emotions using their whole body. What could they do to show happy, sad, scared, tired, angry, and surprised?

Note: If the children seem to enjoy this activity, extend it by turning it into a game of charades. **S** **W**

Invite a group of four children to make "body shapes" on the floor. Challenge the children to form a line, circle, triangle, and square with all group members participating in the creation of each shape. **S**

Divide the children into pairs. Show them how to "mirror" the other person by doing what they do. Invite the children to take turns being the Mover and the Mirror. **W**

No Materials

Invite the children to explore a few kid-friendly yoga poses, or asanas (AH-sah-nahs). Throughout this activity, encourage the children to relax as they breathe slowly and deeply.

- **Butterfly** – Sit on the floor and place the bottoms of your feet together. Sit up straight and tall, hold onto your feet or ankles, and let your knees drop to the floor. Imagine that you have beautiful wings like a butterfly.

- **Cat Stretch** – Kneel on all fours in a "table position" (keep your back straight). Drop your head and arch your back like a cat. Hold for a count of five then return to the table position.

- **Dog Stretch** – Begin in the table position as described above. Raise your head, look at the ceiling, and drop your belly toward the floor. Hold for a count of five then return to the table position.

Note: You may want to combine the cat and dog stretches, alternating between the two. Ⓢ Ⓦ

Invite the children to use their bodies to sound like rain. Ask the children to sit in a circle with their knees bent and their feet on the floor. Begin by rubbing the palms of your hands together. Going around the circle, each child repeats the motion and continues to do it until the Leader (teacher) changes it. Perform each action as described below:

- **Sprinkling Rain** – Rub palms of hands together quickly.

- **Light Rain** – Snap fingers or rapidly tap fingertips on the floor.

- **Heavy Rain** – Quickly tap hands on thighs.

- **Thunder** – Rapidly stomp feet on the floor.

(To end the storm, repeat the steps in reverse order.) Ⓦ

Hoops

The children will surely enjoy this fun and friendly stretching activity! Have 6-8 the children stand in a circle. Hang a hoop on the arm of one child, then ask the children to hold hands. The objective is for the children to pass the hoop all the way around the circle without letting go of each other's hands. **S**

Provide each child with a hoop. Challenge the children to try spinning their hoops on the floor (like coins on a table).

Note: This may not seem like a stability activity at first glance; however, your body must twist (with balance) as you attempt to spin the hoop. **S**

Encourage each child to place his/her hands on opposite sides of a hoop. Lead children through a variety of stretching movements using their hoops (e.g., lunge, bend, twist). Allow the children some time to freely explore other movements with the hoops when you are done stretching together. **S** **W**

Caution: Do this activity in a large, open space so the children can move about safely.

Jump Ropes

Provide each pair of children with a jump rope. Encourage the children to practice turning the jump rope to a rhythm. Chant rhymes together or play music in the background. (S) (W)

Lay several jump ropes on the floor end to end to form a long straight line. Encourage the children to frog jump, bear walk (shown below), and crab walk down the pathway without touching the rope. (S)

Give each child a jump rope. Invite the children to form shapes on the floor with their jump ropes, then perform various movements to develop stability inside and outside the shapes they have made. (S) (W)

Invite the children to do the Limbo. Divide the children into groups of four. Two of the children should hold a jump rope tightly at head height, while the other two children limbo under the rope. Remind the children to lower the rope just a bit after both children have gone under it. Once the rope is lowered to about waist height, the children should switch roles (the rope holders should now limbo). How low can you go?

Note: As an extra-special touch, you may want to play a recording of "The Limbo" in the background. (W)

For each child, cut a 2–3 foot segment of rope or clothesline. Invite the children to perform various stretches while holding their ropes in both hands. They could sway from side to side, reach up high, bend to the floor, and so on. (S) (W)

Let's Get Fit!

Manipulative Skills

Manipulative
Rolling, Bouncing, & Volleying

Help children begin to develop their hand-eye coordination skills with these fun activities!

Roll and Bounce
(tune: "The Farmer in the Dell")

Roll the ball to me.
Please roll the ball to me.
Then I'll roll it back to you –
Please roll the ball to me.

Bounce the ball to me.
Please bounce the ball to me.
Then I'll bounce it back to you –
Please bounce the ball to me.

 ### Hoops

Rolling Activity - Divide children into pairs and give each pair a hoop. Model how to roll a hoop forward along its edge. Invite the children to roll the hoops to their partners. Ⓢ

Rolling Activity - Provide each child with a hoop. The objective is to roll the hoop forward and run to catch it. Once the children have practiced this skill, they may want to try rolling the hoop forward but with a backwards spin so it rolls back to them. Ⓢ

Let's Get Fit!

Balls

Rolling Activity - Divide children into pairs and give each pair a rubber playground ball. Challenge the children to roll the ball to their partners using various body parts (e.g., top of head, nose, elbow, knee). Ⓢ Ⓦ

Rolling Activity - Securely attach a poster or large sheet of construction paper to the wall, close to the floor. The objective is to roll the ball and "hit the target" (poster/paper). Begin by having the children roll the ball from a seated position, then from a standing position.

Note: A heavier ball, such as a basketball, works best for this activity. Ⓢ

Rolling Activity - Set up six "bowling pins" (two-liter soda bottles weighted with sand) in a straight line. Encourage the children to knock down the pins by rolling the ball from a seated position. Rearrange the pins so there are 3 in the back, 2 in the middle, and 1 in front. This time, challenge the children to knock down the pins by rolling the ball from a standing position.

Note: To maximize opportunities for participation, set up several stations of this activity. Ⓢ

Rolling Activity - Provide each pair of children with a ball. Have partners stand side by side, 10–20 feet away from an open wall. One child rolls the ball toward the wall and the other child runs after it. The objective is for the second child to stop the ball with his/her foot before it bounces off the wall and begins to roll back. Switch roles and repeat. Ⓢ

Let's Get Fit!

Balls

Rolling Activity - Have the children sit in a large circle. Place three two-liter soda bottles (weighted with sand) in the middle of the circle. Invite the children to roll one or two balls across the circle and try to knock down the bottles. For a more challenging activity, use three balls and choose three children to stand in the center to block the other children's attempts at knocking the bottles down. Ⓢ Ⓦ

Bouncing Activities

Bouncing a ball with control requires a great deal of practice. When working with young children, use a large bouncing ball whenever possible, such as a rubber playground ball or basketball.

Bouncing Activity - Provide each child with a ball. Model how to hold the ball at chest level, let it drop and bounce, then catch it with two hands. Invite the children to practice this skill several times before moving onto more advanced activities. Ⓢ Ⓦ

Bouncing Activity - Give each child a ball. Hold up a number card from 1–5. Encourage the children to drop and catch their balls as many times as the number written on the card. Ⓢ Ⓦ

Balls

Bouncing Activity - Allow the children several opportunities to practice dribbling a ball with both hands. *Dribbling* is a repetitive bouncing motion (no "catch" step between bounces). First, have the children experiment dribbling a ball with both hands in a flat, somewhat overly-extended position. Next, suggest they try dribbling the ball with their fingertips. Which hand position gives you more control over the ball? *(fingertips)* Once the children feel comfortable dribbling the ball in place, they may choose to try dribbling the ball while walking forward. Ⓢ Ⓦ

Bouncing Activity - Provide each child with a ball and a hoop. Invite the children to stand outside their hoops and bounce/catch or dribble the balls inside the hoops. Some children may want to count the number of times they can bounce the ball in the hoop. Ⓢ

Bouncing Activity - Talk about traffic lights and what the colors mean. Provide each child with a ball. Invite the children to bounce/catch or dribble their balls when you say, "Green light!" When you say, "Red light!" the children should catch their balls with two hands. Ⓢ

Bouncing Activity - Lay two jump ropes on the floor about two feet apart and parallel to each other. Challenge the children to bounce/catch or dribble a ball as they travel down the pathway. Ⓢ

Bouncing Activity - Divide the children into pairs. Have partners stand about five feet apart. Model how to do a "bounce pass" – hold ball at chest, bounce ball toward partner (at about half the distance), partner catches ball with both hands. Provide several opportunities for the children to practice the bounce pass. Ⓢ Ⓦ

Rolling, Bouncing, & Volleying

Balls

Volleying Activities

Volleying is repeatedly striking a ball in the air before it touches the ground. To help ensure the children's success and increase their comfort with this skill, use punching balls with the elastic band removed or inflatable beach balls for the following activities.

Volleying Activity - Provide each child with a ball. Model how to toss the ball into the air, then strike it with both hands (palms open) so it goes up again. When the ball comes back down, the children should catch it with two hands. After practicing this several times, encourage each child to try repeatedly volleying the ball into the air. Ⓢ Ⓦ

Volleying Activity - Divide children into pairs and give each pair a ball. Invite the children to volley the balls to their partners. Once the children feel comfortable with this skill, challenge them to count how many times they can volley the ball without letting it touch the ground. Ⓢ Ⓦ

Volleying Activity - Invite the children to explore volleying a ball with various parts of the body. Can they volley the ball with their head? Can they volley it with their knee? How many different body parts can they use to volley the ball? Ⓢ Ⓦ

Volleying Activity - Play a simple version of volleyball. Set up a low net. Divide children into pairs and give each pair a ball. Encourage the children to volley the ball to each other over the net.

Note: If you don't have a net, string a folded bedsheet from wall to wall inside your classroom. Ⓢ

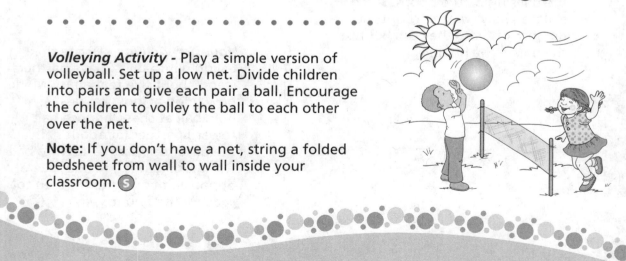

Parachutes

Rolling Activity - The children will surely "exercise" their cooperation skills in this challenging activity. Have the children stand around a parachute and hold it with palms down (thumbs below). Place a medium-sized ball on the parachute. Encourage the children to sing the song below as they roll the ball in a continuous circle along the edge of the parachute. Ⓦ

Round and Round

(tune: "The Wheels on the Bus")

A rolling ball goes round and round,
Round and round, round and round.
A rolling ball goes round and round –
Round and round.

Volleying Activity - Use a parachute to add a new twist to volleying a ball. Have the children stand around a parachute and hold it with palms down (thumbs below). Place a beanbag or lightweight ball on the parachute. The objective is to shake the parachute, making the beanbag/ball "bounce" (volley) into the air.

Note: If you use several beanbags and/or balls in various colors, you could pretend that you are mixing up some fruit salad, then enjoy fruit salad for snack that day. Ⓦ

Manipulative
Passing, Tossing, & Throwing

Passing, tossing, and throwing are skills used in many cooperative games.

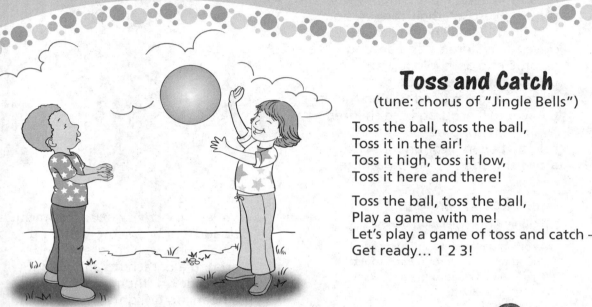

Toss and Catch
(tune: chorus of "Jingle Bells")

Toss the ball, toss the ball,
Toss it in the air!
Toss it high, toss it low,
Toss it here and there!

Toss the ball, toss the ball,
Play a game with me!
Let's play a game of toss and catch –
Get ready… 1 2 3!

Beanbags

Passing Activity - Divide children into two or three groups and provide each group with a beanbag. Play recorded music as the children pass the beanbag around the circle. When the music stops, the child holding the beanbag should stand up, move in a silly way, then sit back down. Ⓦ

Passing Activity - Form groups of six to eight children and have them stand side by side. Give one child at either end of the line a beanbag. The objective is for the children to pass the beanbag down the line in front of their bodies, then back up the line behind their backs. After several loops around the line, challenge the children to switch directions. Ⓢ Ⓦ

Let's Get Fit!

Beanbags

Passing Activity - Ask the children to sit in a circle. Have the children pass a beanbag around the circle, gently handing it off to the next person. After the beanbag has been passed about 1½ times around the circle, introduce another beanbag into the mix. At the next open opportunity, add one more beanbag. Challenge the children to keep all three beanbags moving around the circle at the same time. Ⓦ

Passing Activity - Have the children sit in a circle and pass three or four different colored beanbags around the circle at the same time. At your signal, the children holding the beanbags should stand up. Invite each standing child, in turn, to energetically announce the color of the beanbag he/she is holding. After each child identifies the color, the rest of the children should repeat the color two times (like a cheer). Ⓢ Ⓦ

Passing Activity - Form groups of six to eight children and ask them to sit in a circle. Have the children pass a beanbag around the circle as you sing the following song together. Once the song is over, the children should pass the beanbag around the circle in the other direction. Ⓢ Ⓦ

Pass the Beanbag
(tune: "Oh, My Darling Clementine")

Pass the beanbag, pass the beanbag,
Pass the beanbag now to me.
Oh, the song will soon be over –
Change direction won't you please.

Let's Get Fit!

Beanbags

Tossing Activity - Invite each child to toss a beanbag up into the air and catch it with two hands. Some children may also want to try catching the beanbag with one hand. Provide several opportunities for the children to practice these skills. Ⓢ Ⓦ

Toss a Beanbag
(tune: "Yankee Doodle")

Toss a beanbag in the air
And use your hands to catch it.
If you miss, just try again –
It takes a lot of practice!

Tossing Activity - Scatter number cards on the floor with at least five feet between each card. Give each child a beanbag. Encourage the children to move around the room from station to station (card to card). At each station, the children should toss and catch their beanbags as many times as shown on the card. Ⓢ Ⓦ

Tossing Activity - Provide each child with a beanbag. Encourage the children to toss their beanbags from one hand to the other. For example, if you toss the beanbag with your left hand, you would catch it with your right hand (and vice versa). Ⓢ Ⓦ

Tossing Activity - Divide children into pairs. Give each pair a hoop and a beanbag. One child should hold the hoop about waist height either "standing up" (vertically) or "lying down" (horizontally). The other child should toss the beanbag through the hoop from a distance at which he/she is comfortable. At your signal, the children should switch roles. Ⓢ Ⓦ

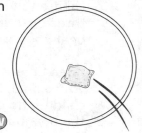

Tossing Activity - Lay one hoop of every available color side by side in the center of the room. (The hoops should touch.) Have the children form a large circle around the hoops. Invite the children to toss matching colored beanbags into the appropriate hoops. Ⓢ Ⓦ

Beanbags

Tossing Activity - Invite the children to try this challenging activity called Flip the Pancake.

Begin by placing a beanbag on the back of one hand. Slide your hands together with pointer fingers touching, thumbs hiding, and palms down. Scoot the beanbag over a bit so it rests in the center of your hands.

Toss the beanbag up into the air, as if you were flipping a pancake. Quickly turn your hands over and catch the beanbag with your hands together, pinkies touching, and palms up. Now toss the beanbag with your palms up and catch it with your palms down. Repeat, each time alternating palms down and palms up.

Note: This task is very difficult, but the children may enjoy giving it a try! If you notice that some children are getting frustrated with this activity, allow them to play another tossing and catching game of their choice. Ⓢ Ⓦ

Tossing Activity - After the children have demonstrated success tossing a beanbag into the air and catching it, challenge them to try one or more of the following "tricks":

- Toss the beanbag into the air as high as it can go, then catch it.

- Toss the beanbag into the air and clap your hands three times before you catch it.

- Toss the beanbag into the air and turn around before you catch it.

- Toss the beanbag into the air, then touch the ground and stand up before you catch it.

- Toss the beanbag into the air in a forward direction and stretch, walk, or run to catch it. Ⓢ

Passing, Tossing, & Throwing

Beanbags

Tossing Activity - Place a few boxes on the floor several feet apart. Ask three or four children to gather around each box, and give each child a different colored beanbag. Have children begin by standing with their toes touching the box. The objective is for each child to toss his/her beanbag into the box with increasing distance. After each successful toss, the child should take one step back.

Note: In order to keep frustration levels low, allow the children to move closer to the box as desired. Ⓢ

Tossing Activity - Divide children into pairs. Have partners stand about three feet apart and face each other. Encourage the children to toss a beanbag back and forth to their partners. At your signal, one child in each pair should take one step backwards. By increasing the distance between the children, the task becomes more challenging. Ⓢ Ⓦ

Throwing Activities

Finding balls that are the "right size" for little hands to grasp is rather difficult, so consider using beanbags for the throwing activities. Beanbags have just enough weight to them (not too heavy, not too light) and are easy for young children to hold.

Throwing Activity - Tossing and throwing are related, but throwing is a more advanced skill. Encourage the children to experiment with various throwing techniques in a large, open outdoor space. Do not correct the children's "form" at this point, but rather guide the children to help them discover more effective throwing techniques. What would happen if you stepped forward as you throw the beanbag? Do you get more control and power when you stand still or step forward as you throw? (Intervene only if the children are throwing directly at the ground.) Eventually encourage the children to try throwing their beanbags "far and hard." Ⓢ Ⓦ

Beanbags

Throwing Activity - As you observe the children, you may find that some of them are ready to try using the proper technique to throw. For these children, model the proper way to throw a beanbag or ball (as explained below) and provide several opportunities for them to practice this skill.

Proper Throwing Technique: Hold the beanbag in your preferred hand and turn the opposite side of your body toward your "target" (where you want the ball to land). Bring your arm way back with the beanbag around the level/height of your ear. In one smooth movement, step forward with the opposite foot (toes pointing toward the target) and "follow through" by releasing the beanbag as you bring your arm forward. Some children may be ready to try following through with their back foot (and thus, their whole body) as they release the beanbag.

Note: Keep in mind that at this age, it's more appropriate for children to freely experiment with throwing, rather than throwing to other children or at teacher-designated targets. Ⓢ

Balls

Passing Activities

For the following three activities, form groups of six to eight children and have them stand in a single file line. Provide each group with a rubber playground ball or an inflatable beach ball.

Passing Activity - Before the game, decide if the children should pass the ball over their heads or through their legs. The first person in each group passes the ball to the next person in the designated way. Once the last person receives the ball, he/she runs with the ball to the front of the line then continues to pass the ball. Ⓢ Ⓦ

Passing Activity - The first person in each group passes the ball over his/her head. When the last person receives the ball, he/she passes the ball back up the line but this time through the legs of the person in front him/her. Once the last person passes the ball, he/she runs to the front of the line. When the ball reaches the first person (who was just the last person), the ball is passed overhead once again. Ⓢ Ⓦ

Passing, Tossing, & Throwing

 ## Balls

Passing Activity - Beginning with the first person in each group, the children twist to the left to pass the ball down the line. When the last person receives the ball he/she passes the ball back up the line, but this time to the right. Once the last person passes the ball, he/she runs to the front of the line. When the ball reaches the first person (who was just the last person), the ball is passed along the left once again. Ⓢ Ⓦ

Tossing Activities

For the following five activities, begin by using inflatable beach balls or punching balls with the elastic band removed. As the children become more successful tossing and catching a ball, invite them to use a smaller (yet soft) ball with which to play.

Tossing Activity - Invite each child to toss a ball up into the air and catch it with two hands. Provide several opportunities for the children to practice this basic skill. Ⓢ Ⓦ

Tossing Activity - Divide children into pairs. Have partners stand about three feet apart and face each other. Encourage the children to toss a ball back and forth to their partners. At your signal, one child in each pair should take one step backwards. By increasing the distance between the children, the task becomes more challenging. Ⓢ Ⓦ

Balls

Tossing Activity - Form groups of four or five children. Have each group stand in a large circle. (The children's fingertips should barely be able to touch.) Encourage the children to toss a ball around the circle. The children may want to count how many times the ball is tossed before it falls to the ground. Ⓢ Ⓦ

Tossing Activity - Have the children stand in a large circle. Call out a child's name and toss the ball to him/her. That child should then call out another child's name and toss the ball to that person. Repeat until all of the children have a chance to catch and toss the ball. Ⓢ

Tossing Activity - Try this variation of "basket" ball. Invite the children to toss a ball into a laundry basket. Adjust the distance from the basket to meet the needs of each child.

Note: To maximize opportunities for participation, set up several stations of this activity. Ⓢ

 ## Other Materials

Passing Activity - Invite the children to sit in a circle. Sing the following song together as you pass two plastic play foods (one fruit and one vegetable) around the circle. At the end of the song, the child holding the fruit should name his/her favorite fruit, and the child holding the vegetable should name his/her favorite vegetable. Continue to play until all of the children have shared their favorite fruit and/or vegetable. Ⓢ Ⓦ

I Am Growing
(tune: "Twinkle, Twinkle, Little Star")

I am growing every day.
Watch me learn and watch me play.
Healthy foods are fun to eat.
Fruits and veggies are a treat.
Exercise and lots of rest
Help me be my very best!

Passing, Tossing, & Throwing

 ## Other Materials

Passing Activity - Ask the children to sit in a circle. Encourage the children to talk about things we should do to help us stay healthy (e.g., drink lots of water, eat healthy foods, brush your teeth, exercise, wash your hands, take a bath).

Sing the following song together as you pass two or three new bath sponges around the circle. The children who are holding the sponges on the last "Hooray!" should stand, run around the circle, and then sit back in their spots. Continue to play until all of the children have had a turn. ⑤ⓦ

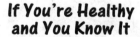

If You're Healthy and You Know It
(tune: "If You're Happy and You Know It")

If you're healthy and you know it –
Shout "Hooray!" *(Hooray!)*

If you're healthy and you know it –
Shout "Hooray!" *(Hooray!)*

If you're healthy and you know it,
Then you really ought to show it.

If you're healthy and you know it –
Shout "Hooray!" *(Hooray!)*

Tossing Activity - Set out several plastic cones. (Be sure the cones are spread far apart.) Encourage the children to toss hoops over the cones from varying distances.

Note: If you do not have plastic cones, you can use two-liter soda bottles weighted with sand. ⑤

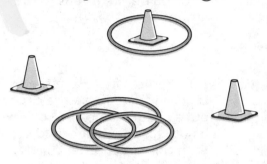

Tossing Activity - Place several large plastic bowls on the floor. Give each child a disposable cup filled with pom-poms or cotton balls. Have two or three children stand around each bowl about three feet away. The objective is to toss the pom-poms or cotton balls into the bowls. ⑤ⓦ

Tossing Activity - Provide each child with a large craft feather. Invite the children to toss their feathers high into the air and catch them with one hand. ⑤ⓦ

Other Materials

Tossing Activity - Invite the children to have a Pillow Toss! Explain that young children need about twelve hours of sleep to stay healthy. Count with the children from 1-12 as you point to the numbers around a clock.

Have the children stand in a large circle. (The children's fingertips should barely be able to touch.) Sing the following song together as you toss a travel-sized pillow around the circle. At the end of the song, the child holding the pillow should call out another child's name. Both children should run one full time around the circle then sit in the other child's spot. Continue to play until all of the children have had a turn. S W

Get a Lot of Rest

(tune: "The Farmer in the Dell")

Oh, get a lot of rest.
Oh, get a lot of rest.
To feel refreshed and do your best
Yes, get a lot of rest!

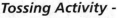

Tossing Activity - Provide each child with a scarf. Invite the children to toss their scarves high into the air and catch them with one hand. S W

Tossing Activity - Write each child's name on the bottom of a sturdy paper plate. Encourage the children to toss their paper plates like flying discs. The children should run to collect their plates and repeat several times. S W

Tossing Activity - Give each child a sheet of newspaper to crumple tightly into a ball. Place a new or sanitized trash can in the center of the room. Explain that *littering*, or throwing trash on the ground, is a form of pollution and is bad for the earth. Have children toss their "trash" (newspaper balls) into the trash can. Invite the children to scatter the paper balls around the room and then toss them back into the can. S W

Manipulative
Kicking

Kicking activities help children develop coordination, balance, and timing.

Kick the Ball

Kick with your left.
Kick with your right.
Kick the ball hard
With all of your might.

Kick the ball here.
Kick the ball there.
Kick the ball low
Or high in the air.

When you first introduce kicking, use slightly deflated rubber playground balls. As the children begin to demonstrate success with the skill, use fully inflated rubber playground balls and/or soccer balls.

 ## Balls

Kicking can be a challenging skill for many young children. Encourage the children to experiment with various kicking techniques in a large, open outdoor space. Do not correct the children's "form" at this point, but rather guide the children to help them discover more effective kicking techniques. Can you kick with the top of your foot? inside of your foot? outside of your foot? (Intervene only if the children are kicking with the tips of their toes.) Eventually encourage the children to try kicking their balls "far and hard." Ⓢ Ⓦ

Balls

After giving the children time to explore kicking on their own, model how to kick with your *instep* (top of the foot between the toes and ankle). To help the children remember this kicking technique, tell them to kick the ball "with their shoelaces." Provide several opportunities for the children to practice this skill.

Note: Some children may be ready to try taking two or more steps away from the ball, then moving toward the ball to kick it. Ⓢ

Divide children into pairs. Give each pair a ball and have the children stand about ten feet away from their partners. Encourage each child to kick the ball with control (aim toward partner, keep the ball on the ground, don't kick too hard). When the ball is returned, each child should stop the ball with his/her foot. Ⓢ Ⓦ

Encourage the children to practice "dribbling" a ball with their feet. Dribbling requires short, controlled kicks using the inside or outside of your feet to move the ball forward.

Note: You often kick with alternating feet, but not necessarily. Ⓢ Ⓦ

Talk about traffic lights and what the colors mean. Provide each child with a ball. Invite the children to dribble the balls using their feet when you say "Green light!" When you say "Red light!" the children should stop their balls with one foot. Ⓢ

Kicking

 ## Balls

Place boxes in gradually decreasing sizes against the wall with the openings facing out (not up). Invite the children to try to kick a ball into each "goal" (box), beginning with the largest box. Ⓢ

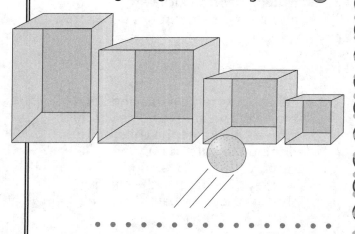

Invite three children to stand in the center of the room. Have the rest of the children stand in a large circle around those children. (The children's fingertips should barely be able to touch.) The objective is for the children inside the circle to try to kick the ball out of the circle, while the rest of the children use their feet to try to keep the ball inside the circle.

Note: You may want to discuss good sportsmanship before you play this game (e.g., safe kicks, teamwork, positive attitudes). Ⓦ

 ## Beanbags

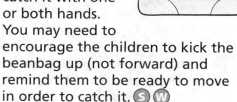

Have each child balance a beanbag on the top of his/her preferred foot, kick it high into the air, and catch it with one or both hands. You may need to encourage the children to kick the beanbag up (not forward) and remind them to be ready to move in order to catch it. Ⓢ Ⓦ

Designate a starting point and ending point that are significantly far apart from each other. The objective is for the children to kick the beanbag from "point A" to "point B."

Note: The children should not be expected to arrive at the goal with one kick, but rather several short kicks. Ⓢ

Beanbags

Place boxes in gradually decreasing sizes against the wall with the openings facing out (not up). Invite the children to try to kick a beanbag into each "goal" (box), beginning with the largest box. Ⓢ

Divide children into pairs. Give each pair a hoop and a beanbag. One child should hold the hoop about waist height either "standing up" (vertically) or "lying down" (horizontally). The other child should try to kick the beanbag through the hoop from a distance at which he/she is comfortable. At your signal, the children should switch roles. Ⓢ Ⓦ

Lay two jump ropes on the floor about five feet apart and parallel to each other. Have the children stand about ten feet away from the jump ropes. Challenge each child to kick a beanbag so it lands between the two ropes. Ⓢ

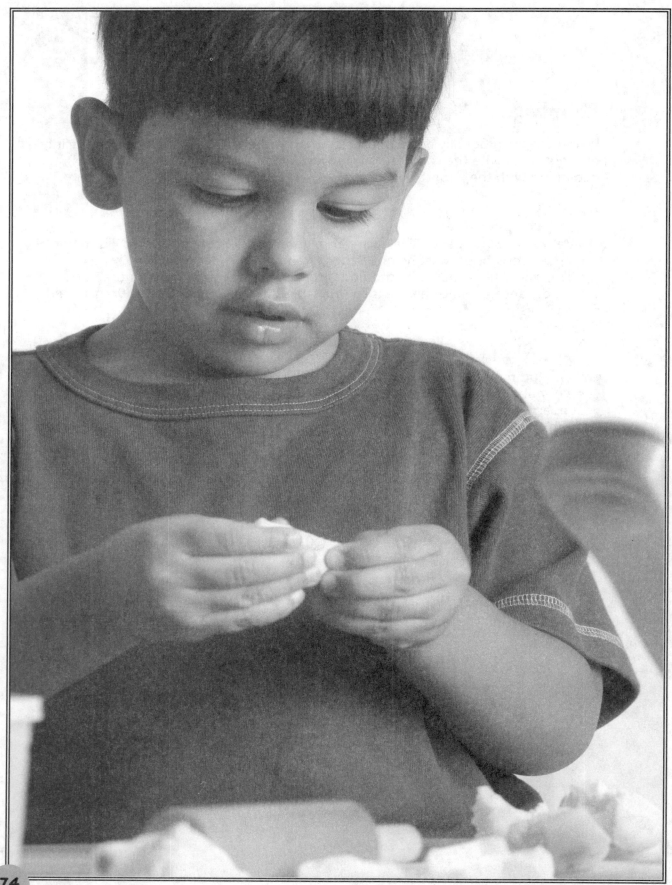

Let's Get Fit!

Fine Motor Skills

Fine Motor
Tearing, Cutting, & Gluing

These fun activities develop "finger skills" – a necessary prerequisite for writing.

I Can Cut

I cut paper that's green.
I cut paper that's blue.
I cut paper that's full of
Red polka dots, too.

I cut out a circle.
I cut out a square.
I cut out a heart
To show someone I care.

Tearing, Cutting & Gluing

Invite the children to tear regular and irregular shapes from various colors of paper. They may also choose to glue the shapes onto large sheets of construction paper to make collages.

Using a digital camera, take a picture of each child. Print off the pictures and glue a piece of posterboard to the back of each picture. Set aside and allow the pictures to dry overnight. On the back of each picture, draw simple "puzzle lines," dividing the picture into four pieces. Invite the children to cut their pictures along the lines to create their very own puzzles!

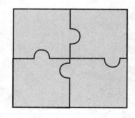

Tearing, Cutting & Gluing

One way to keep your body healthy is to eat foods that are good for you. Encourage the children to share what they know about healthy food and junk food. Explain that "junk food" is bad for our bodies because it has a lot of sugar, salt, and/or fat. Invite the children to tear or cut pictures of healthy foods from magazines and glue the pictures onto paper plates.

Draw straight and curvy lines on a sheet of plain paper and make several copies. Invite the children to cut along the lines to help develop their cutting skills.

Have each child cut several circles, triangles, or squares of various sizes from construction paper. Encourage the children to arrange their shapes in order from biggest to smallest.

Note: Each child should choose only one shape to cut out and order.

Set out large sheets of construction paper, glue, and variety of craft materials (e.g., pom-poms, felt, paper, chenille stems, ribbon). Invite the children to create collages by gluing the materials onto paper.

Draw two of each of the following shapes (one big, one small) on a sheet of plain paper: circle, square, triangle, and rectangle. Make several copies of the paper for the children to cut. Once all of the shapes have been cut out, encourage each child to sort the shapes in several different ways.

Set up a "cutting pool" in your classroom. Bring in a small plastic children's pool. Fill the pool with lots of paper in all shapes, sizes, colors, and patterns. Place two pairs of child-safe scissors in a container next to the pool. When children are in the pool, they may tear or cut paper in any way they choose. Remind the children to follow these three simple rules:
(1) Only two children in the pool at a time.
(2) Keep the paper inside the pool.
(3) Make safe choices.

Fine Motor
Stacking & Pouring

Stacking and pouring are fine motor skills that young children utilize each and every day.

Stack and Pour
(tune: "Row, Row, Row Your Boat")

Stack, stack, stack some blocks,
Stack them really high.
Make a tower with your blocks
That reaches to the sky.

Pour, pour, pour a drink,
Pour some in your cup.
Don't worry if you start to spill
We can clean it up.

 ## Stacking & Pouring

Invite the children to freely explore building with blocks. As the children are playing, ask questions to encourage them to talk about their block creations. What are you building? How many blocks tall is it? Is it easier to stack a large block on top of a small block, or a small block on top of a large block? What shape is this block?

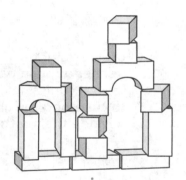

Divide children into pairs. One child should stack ten blocks on top of each other to form a tower. Once the tower is complete, the other child should take the blocks down one block at a time. Switch roles and repeat.

Encourage the children to look around the room for objects that can be stacked on top of each other. Discuss several possibilities together, then invite the children to test out their ideas.

Stacking & Pouring

Display a picture of a triangle and a picture of a pyramid (like those built in Egypt). Talk about how the two shapes are similar and different. Give each child ten small disposable cups (3-ounce bathroom cups). Challenge the children to stack all ten cups so it looks like a pyramid. Assist the children as needed by providing clues and examples, but encourage them to try to solve this pyramid puzzle on their own.

• • • • • • • • • •

While playing at the sand table or in the sandbox, encourage the children to explore filling and dumping containers of various shapes and sizes.

• • • • • • • • • •

Set out a small plastic pitcher of colored water, several containers of various sizes, and a few funnels. Encourage the children to pour water from one container to the next. As the children are exploring, talk about liquids. Explain that a liquid flows to take the shape of its container.

At snack time, invite the children to pour water into their own cups to drink. Be sure to provide the children with small plastic pitchers of water… and have plenty of paper towels on hand!

• • • • • • • • • •

Take the children outside on a warm day. Designate a starting line and a finishing line, about 20 feet apart. Place large buckets of water on the starting line and smaller empty buckets on the finishing line. Divide children into small groups and ask each group to stand in a single file line behind a large bucket. The objective is to work together to carry the water from one bucket to the other using disposable cups. (Only one child from each group may travel at a time.)

Note: You may want to write a note home to families before this activity so the children can dress appropriately and bring an extra set of clothes in case they get too wet.

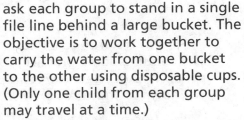

Fine Motor
Exploring & Creating

Provide several opportunities for young children to explore and create in fun and meaningful ways.

Use Your Imagination

Squish it like a pancake,
Or roll it in a ball.
You can use some playdough
To make anything at all!

Paint a little picture,
Create a craft or two.
Use your imagination
And just see what you can do!

Exploring & Creating

Set out two plastic bowls, leave one empty and fill the other with pom-poms or cotton balls. Encourage the children to transfer the pom-poms or cotton balls one at a time to the empty bowl using a spring-type clothespin.

Invite the children to explore lacing cards. This requires some practice, so assist the children as needed. *(Directions for making your own lacing cards are listed below.)*

Directions: Cut shapes out of heavy posterboard. Use a hole punch to make a series of holes around each shape. For each lacing card, tie a string through one hole to anchor it. (Be sure the string is long enough to reach around the shape twice.) Wrap the loose end of each string with masking tape to create a "lacing needle."

Exploring & Creating

Set out several colors of playdough, assorted cookie cutters, toy rolling pins, and so forth. Invite the children to create playdough designs and sculptures.

Invite the children to make and explore goop. Give each child a disposable bowl, ¼ cup cornstarch, and about 3 tablespoons of water. Talk about what the cornstarch feels like before adding the water. Have the children add water to the cornstarch little by little and mix it with their hands. If the mixture seems too dry, add a few more drops of water until it reaches the desired consistency (can roll into a ball, but flows like liquid in palm of hand). Encourage the children to experiment with the goop as desired.

Spread a thick layer of sand or salt in a shallow baking pan. Have the children draw shapes, numerals, or letters in the sand/salt with their fingers.

Note: Remind the children not to rub their eyes when using sand or salt.

Set out a few puzzles with varying degrees of difficulty on a table. Encourage the children to work cooperatively with a partner to assemble a puzzle of their choice.

Set out a free-standing unbreakable mirror, white construction paper, and drawing materials. Invite the children to draw self-portraits after observing themselves in the mirror.

Exploring & Creating

Provide each child with a large sheet of construction paper. Invite the children to practice tracing both hands with a crayon, then decorate as desired.

Note: Be sure to use crayons, not markers, for this activity.

· · · · · · · · · · · · · · · ·

Draw lines on a large paper plate to create six equal sections. Color each section of the plate a different color. Gather six wooden spring-type clothespins. Color each clothespin a different color to match the colors on the plate. Have the children clip the clothespins to the appropriate sections of the plate.

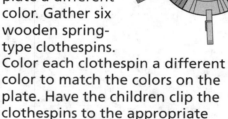

· · · · · · · · · · · · · · · ·

Lay a large sheet of white butcher paper on the floor and set out a variety of art materials. Invite the children to work together to create a class mural. After the children finish, title it "Our Marvelous Mural" and hang it at the children's eye level.

Give each child a sheet of finger-paint paper and set out red, yellow, blue, and white finger paints. Invite the children to mix the colors to create new colors. As the children explore, encourage them to talk about their color discoveries (e.g., red + yellow = orange).

· · · · · · · · · · · · · · · ·

Encourage the children to create sculptures out of foam packing peanuts and chenille stems. Their sculptures can be models of things that really exist or created from their own imaginations. Invite the children to talk about their creations once everyone has finished.

Exploring & Creating

Everyone's fingerprints are different, which is just one way we are all unique! Encourage each child to look closely at the pad of his/her pointer finger. Explain that the swirls they see are called *fingerprints*. Show the children how to rock each finger on a washable-ink pad, then push it down firmly on paper to make a clear print. The children can use magnifying glasses to examine their fingerprints and the fingerprints of others. When finished invite the children to design fingerprint critters with fine-point markers.

Special and Unique
(tune: "If You're Happy
and You Know It")

I am special and unique, yes it's true.
I am special and unique and so are you.
We're as different as can be,
But both special can't you see –
I am special and unique and so are you.

Set out bowls of tempera paint and a variety of unusual painting tools, such as twigs, leaves, pinecones, pieces of yarn, cotton balls, craft feathers, and sponges. Invite the children to paint with one or more of the materials to create their very own masterpieces! Encourage the children to explore different movements and colors of paint as they work on their creations.

Let's Get Fit!

Resources & Reproducibles

National Standards for Physical Education

Designing developmentally appropriate movement experiences for young children may seem insignificant, but it is quite the contrary. The following descriptions were taken directly from the *National Standards for Physical Education* (NASPE, 2004). After reading the goals of a quality physical education, you will understand why promoting healthy habits and an appreciation for fitness is crucial during the early childhood years.

Standard 1 – Demonstrates competency in motor skills and movement patterns needed to perform a variety of physical activities.

The intent of this standard is development of the physical skills needed to enjoy participation in physical activities. Mastering movement fundamentals establishes a foundation to facilitate continued motor skill acquisition and gives students the capacity for successful and advanced levels of performance to further the likelihood of participation on a daily basis. In the primary years, students develop maturity and versatility in the use of fundamental motor skills (e.g., running, skipping, throwing, striking) that are further refined, combined, and varied during the middle school years. These motor skills, now having evolved into specialized skills (e.g., a specific dance step, chest pass; catching with a glove, or the use of a specific tactic), are used in increasingly complex movement environments through the middle school years. On the basis of interest and ability, high school students select a few activities for regular participation within which more advanced skills are mastered. In preparation for adulthood, students acquire the skills to participate in a wide variety of leisure and work-related physical activities.

Standard 2 – Demonstrates understanding of movement concepts, principles, strategies, and tactics as they apply to the learning and performance of physical activities.

The intent of this standard is facilitation of learners' ability to use cognitive information to understand and enhance motor skill acquisition and performance. It enhances the ability to use the mind to control or direct one's performance. This includes the application of concepts from disciplines such as motor learning and development, sport psychology and sociology, and biomechanics and exercise physiology. It includes, for example, increasing force production through the summation of forces, knowing the effects of anxiety on performance, and understanding the principle of specificity of training. Knowledge of these concepts and principles and of how to apply them enhances the likelihood of independent learning and therefore more regular and effective participation in physical activity. In the lower elementary grades, emphasis is placed on establishing a movement vocabulary and applying introductory concepts. Through the upper elementary and middle school years, an emphasis is placed on applying and generalizing these concepts to real-life physical activity situations. In high school, emphasis is placed on students independently and routinely using a wide variety of increasingly complex concepts. By graduation, the student has developed sufficient knowledge and ability to independently use his/her knowledge to acquire new skills while continuing to refine existing ones.

Standard 3 - Participates regularly in physical activity.

The intent of this standard is establishment of patterns of regular participation in meaningful physical activity. This standard connects what is done in the physical education class with the lives of students outside of the classroom. Although participation within the physical education class is important, what the student does outside the physical education class is critical to developing an active, healthy lifestyle that has the potential to help prevent a variety of health problems among future generations of adults. Students make use of the skills and knowledge learned in physical education class as they engage in regular physical activity outside of the physical education class. They demonstrate effective self-management skills that enable them to participate in physical activity on a regular basis. Voluntary participation often develops from the initial enjoyment that is derived from the activity coupled with the requisite skills needed for participation. As students develop an awareness of the relationships between activity and its immediate and identifiable effects on the body, regular participation in physical activity enhances the physical and psychological health of the body, social opportunities and relationships, and quality of life. Students are more likely to participate if they have opportunities to develop interests that are personally meaningful to them. Young children learn to enjoy physical activity yet also learn that a certain level of personal commitment and earnest work is required to reap the benefits from their participation. They partake in developmentally appropriate activities that help them develop movement competence and should be encouraged to participate in moderate to vigorous physical activity and unstructured play. As students get older, the structure of activity tends to increase and the opportunities for participation in different types of activity increase outside of the physical education class. Attainment of this standard encourages participation commensurate with contemporary recommendations regarding the type of activity as well as the frequency, duration, and intensity of participation believed to support and sustain good health.

Standard 4 – Achieves and maintains a health-enhancing level of physical fitness.

The intent of this standard is development of students' knowledge, skills, and willingness to accept responsibility for personal fitness, leading to an active, healthy lifestyle. Students develop higher levels of basic fitness and physical competence as needed for many work situations and active leisure participation. Health-related fitness components include cardiorespiratory endurance, muscular strength and endurance, flexibility, and body composition. Expectations for improvement of students' fitness levels should be established on a personal basis, taking into account variation in entry levels and the long-term goal of achieving health-related levels of fitness based on criterion-referenced standards. Students progress in their ability to participate in moderate to vigorous physical activities that address each component of health-related fitness. Moreover, students become more skilled in their ability to plan, perform, and monitor physical activities appropriate for developing physical fitness. For elementary children, the emphasis is on an awareness of fitness components and having fun while participating in health-enhancing activities that promote physical fitness. Middle school students gradually acquire a greater understanding of the fitness components, the ways each is developed and maintained, and the importance of each in overall fitness. Secondary students are able to design and develop an appropriate personal fitness program that enables them to achieve health-related levels of fitness.

Standard 5 – Exhibits responsible personal and social behavior that respects self and others in physical activity settings.

The intent of this standard is achievement of self-initiated behaviors that promote personal and group success in activity settings. These include safe practices, adherence to rules and procedures, etiquette, cooperation and teamwork, ethical behavior, and positive social interaction. Key to this standard is developing respect for individual similarities and differences through positive interaction among participants in physical activity. Similarities and differences include characteristics of culture, ethnicity, motor performance, disabilities, physical characteristics (e.g., strength, size, shape), gender, age, race, and socio-economic status. Achievement of this standard in the lower elementary grades begins with recognition of classroom rules, procedures, and safety. In the upper elementary levels, children learn to work independently, with a partner, and in small groups. Throughout elementary school, students begin to recognize individual similarities and differences and participate cooperatively in physical activity. In middle school, adolescents identify the purpose of rules and procedures and become involved in decision-making processes to establish the rules and procedures that guide specific activity situations. They participate cooperatively in physical activity with persons of diverse characteristics and backgrounds. High school students initiate responsible behavior, function independently and responsibly, and positively influence the behavior of others in physical activity settings. They participate with all people, avoid and resolve conflicts, recognize the value of diversity in physical activity, and develop strategies for inclusion of others. High school students begin to understand how adult work and family roles and responsibilities affect their decisions about physical activity and how physical activity, preferences, and opportunities change over time.

Standard 6 – Values physical activity for health, enjoyment, challenge, self-expression, and/or social interaction.

The intent of this standard is development of an awareness of the intrinsic values and benefits of participation in physical activity that provides personal meaning. Physical activity provides opportunities for self-expression and social interaction and can be enjoyable, challenging, and fun. These benefits develop self-confidence and promote a positive self-image, thereby enticing people to continue participation in activity throughout the life span. Elementary children derive pleasure from movement sensations and experience challenge and joy as they sense a growing competence in movement ability. At the middle school level, participation in physical activity provides important opportunities for challenge, social interaction, and group membership, as well as opportunities for continued personal growth in physical skills and their applied settings. Participation at the high school level continues to provide enjoyment and challenge as well as opportunities for self-expression and social interaction. As a result of these intrinsic benefits of participation, students will begin to actively pursue lifelong physical activities that meet their own needs.

Reprinted with permission from *Moving Into the Future: National Standards for Physical Education, 2nd Edition* (2004), from the National Association for Sport and Physical Education (NASPE), 1900 Association Drive, Reston, Virginia 20191-1598.

Large Muscle Skills
Activity Variation Guide

How to Use This Guide:

- Select a skill focus and the material(s) used.
  Example: *bounce a ball*

- Select one or more effort variations.
  Example: *bounce a ball with a steady rhythm*

- Select one or more space variations.
  Example: *bounce a ball with a steady rhythm between two jump ropes*

- You may add more variations, as desired (role in activity, size of movement, etc.).

Skill Focus

Locomotor	Stability	Manipulative
traveling (walk, march, run hop, gallop, leap, stomp, tiptoe, slide-step, skip) chasing & fleeing	balancing jumping & landing dancing bending twisting lunging	rolling bouncing volleying passing tossing throwing kicking

Effort Variations

Speed	Rhythm	Intensity/Force
slow medium fast ------- accelerating decelerating	free-flowing steady	low (light) moderate high (strong)

Space Variations

Directions	Level/Height	Pathway	Relationship
forwards backwards sideways up down right left clockwise counterclockwise	low middle high	straight curved zigzag	between beside around through over under in front of behind near

Other Variations

Material(s) Used

Role in Activity

Size of Movement

Body Part(s)

Reproduce numeral cards to use with activities as needed.

1

2

3

4

Let's Get Fit!

Reproduce numeral cards to use with activities as needed.

5

6

7

8

Let's Get Fit!

© HighReach Learning®, Inc.

Reproduce numeral cards to use with activities as needed.

9

10

11

12

Let's Get Fit!

Reproduce shape cards to use with activities as needed.

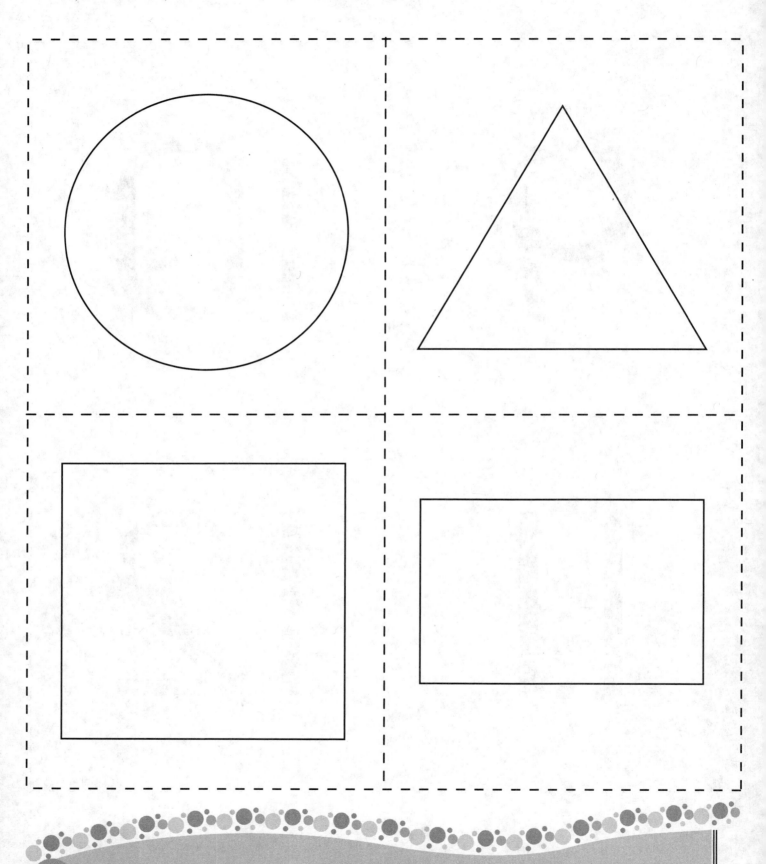

Let's Get Fit!

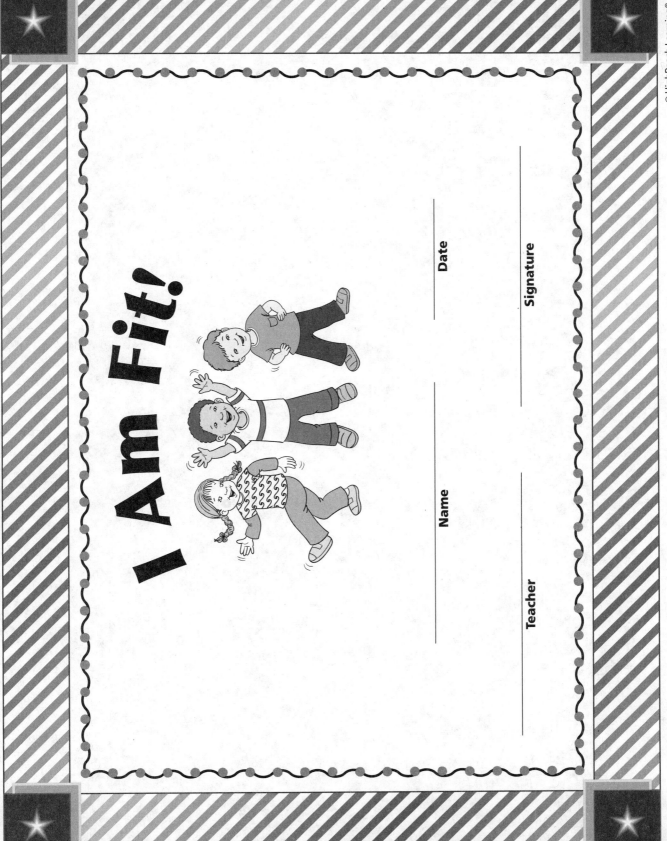

I Am Fit!

Name _____

Teacher _____

Date _____

Signature _____